Michael
Jackson
1958–2009

'73

"My mother used to wake me up at 3 in the morning: 'Michael, he's on TV, he's on TV,'" Jackson once recalled. "I'd run to the TV, and James Brown would be on. I said, 'That's what I want to do.'"

TABLE OF CONTENTS

4 | GALLERY
From Jackson 5 cherub to eccentric
adult, image was everything

32 | SUPERSTAR
How the King of Pop moonwalked
to global fame

42 | FAMOUS FRIENDS
The stars (Macaulay Culkin, Liz Taylor,
Princess Diana) aligned with Michael

52 | GROWING UP
Little MJ had the voice, the steps and
more charm than a bucket of puppies

62 | THINGS GET WEIRD
Llamas, pythons and surgery! Oh, my!

66 | NEVERLAND
A peek at the the quirky star's
Oz-like California retreat

70 | IS THAT YOU?
The changing face of Michael Jackson
through the years

74 | FAMILY MAN
He married the King's daughter and
became a dad, all in his own unusual way

84 | ON TRIAL
Accusations damaged his
reputation—and his psyche

88 | A SUDDEN LOSS
Fans from Buenos Aires to Beirut
mourned a man with global appeal

94 | FAREWELL
Remembering Michael Joseph Jackson

Long Live the King

Stunning talent, childhood stardom, *Thriller,* Bubbles the chimp, Neverland, scandal, marriage (to Elvis's daughter), kids, veils and, always, always, headlines. "There will be a lot written about what came next in Michael's life, but for me all of that is just noise," said Quincy Jones, his friend and collaborator. "I promise you in 50, 75, 100 years, what will be remembered is the music. It's no accident that almost three decades later, no matter where I go in the world, in every club and karaoke bar, like clockwork, you hear 'Billie Jean,' 'Beat It,' 'Wanna Be Startin' Something,' 'Rock with You' and 'Thriller.'"

'89

"I've always wanted to be able to tell stories, you know, stories that came from my soul," Michael wrote in *Moonwalk,* his 1988 autobiography. "I'd like to tell tales to move . . . souls and transform them."

Jackson was exquisitely aware, every moment, of the image he wanted to project. He "is grounded and centered and focused," *Thriller* producer Quincy Jones told PEOPLE in 1987, "and connected to his creative soul."

"He takes a step that you've been doing and then by the time he switches it around, you don't even recognize it," song-and-dance legend Sammy Davis Jr. told PEOPLE in 1984. "Can he tap dance? I don't know. But then again I'd hate to leave my dancing shoes in his vicinity."

66

Michael was always beyond his years. When I first heard him sing Smokey's song 'Who's Lovin' You' at 10 years old, it felt like he had lived the song for 50 years"

—Motown founder Berry Gordy

Which one is not like the others? Michael—yes, he's the one in rhinestones—poses with real Detroit cops before shooting a video with them in 1984.

"I would like to think that I'm an inspiration for the children I meet," Michael wrote in *Moonwalk*. "I want kids to like my music. Their approval means more to me than anyone else's."

Not *everyone* was a fan. Jackson's music, grumbled a 1984 editorial in a Soviet newspaper, is "characteristic of that ill-famed American lifestyle which the USA is trying to foist on the world. [The *Thriller* video] is really fascist, because it forces you to appreciate it like a drug."

"

Often in the past, performers have been tragic figures.... It's so sad. You feel cheated as a fan that you didn't get to watch them evolve as they grew older"

—Michael in *Moonwalk*, which Jacqueline Onassis, an editor at Doubleday, persuaded him to write.

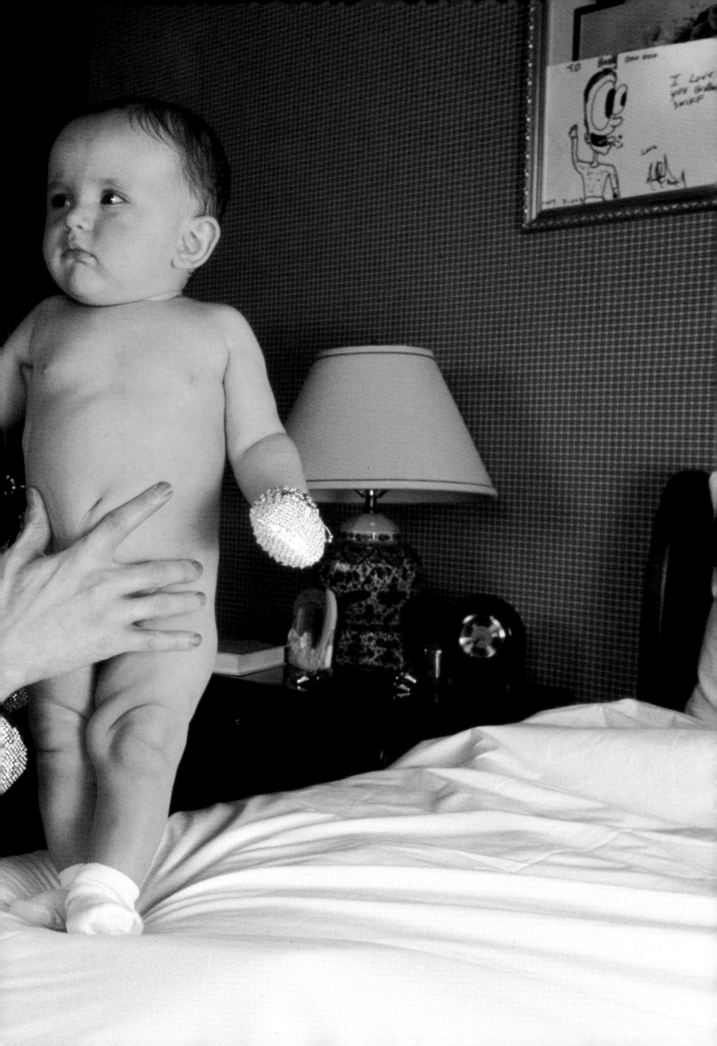

The man in the mirror: "Michael Jackson's passionate refusal to be drawn into the world of sexual experience is as revolutionary a stance for our times as was Elvis Presley's defiant assertion of sexuality in the '50s," author Albert Goldman wrote in PEOPLE in 1984.

> **"**
>
> I'm crazy about monkeys,
> especially chimps. My chimp
> Bubbles is a constant delight. I really
> enjoy taking him with me on
> trips or excursions. He's a wonderful
> distraction and a great pet"
>
> —Michael in *Moonwalk*

An all-Michael conference call, ca. 1991: "I love to create magic—to put something together that's so unusual, so unexpected that it blows people's heads off," he once said. "Something ahead of the times."

"His most remarkable achievement," Albert Goldman wrote in PEOPLE's special Michael Jackson issue in 1984, "is to make his body talk."

"I believe strongly in a higher force, and I'm really thankful for all the blessings," Michael told *Ebony* magazine during his last published interview in 2007.

"He's the only reason I do what I do," says R&B singer Ne-Yo of his idol. "Music sounds the way it sounds today because of Michael."

Michael Jackson

SUPER STAR

THERE WERE POP IDOLS BEFORE HIM—AND MANY SINCE. BUT NO ONE SEIZED THE WORLD STAGE QUITE LIKE THE KING OF POP, WHO FOR A DECADE REDEFINED THE NATURE OF FAME

'84

Man walked on the moon in 1969. Michael Jackson moonwalked in 1983. One of those events so astonished the world that it tore down boundaries, changed societies and spawned a massive cult of hero worship.

Sorry, Neil—in the world of popular culture, the game-changer was Jackson. His breakout performance of "Billie Jean" on the 1983 TV special *Motown 25: Yesterday, Today, Forever*—in which, 3 minutes and 40 seconds into the song, he took four sliding steps backward while appearing to walk forward, an otherwordly move that might as well have been a spe-

cial effect—helped launch Jackson to an unprecedented level of fame, influence and success. In an age before Twitter, Facebook and tabloid TV, Jackson became a true global sensation, transforming the landscapes of music and pop culture, sparking instant fashion trends (in both men's and women's wear) and inspiring a generation of future stars. "He was a pioneer who transcended genre and race," says singer Rob Thomas, one of dozens of artists to trace their careers straight back to Jackson's influence. "He had the most unique talent the world has ever or will ever see."

How big was Jackson? For roughly 10 years,

Jackson (in his signature white rhinestone glove) scooped up an amazing eight Grammys at the '84 awards show.

"Michael stands for something," said Madonna (with Jackson in 1991). "He's a fascinating person."

from 1983 to 1993, he commanded the world's attention like few entertainers before and none since. After the Motown special, sales of his 1983 album *Thriller* skyrocketed on the way to an estimated total of more than 100 million sold—making it one the biggest records in history. Like Sinatra, Elvis and the Beatles before him, Jackson saw his every appearance turn into a mob scene, reducing hordes of fans to Jell-O just by showing up. His extravagant 1984 Victory megatour—for which he lugged a 375-ton stage, 65,000 lbs. of gear and his 5 brothers to 21 cities—was a colossal success.

Jackson became the first African-American artist ever to be featured on MTV, met President Ronald Reagan at the White House, squired Brooke Shields—the fairest damsel in the land—to the Grammys, and wrangled a small army of A-listers to sing 1985's "We Are the World," which he cowrote. Jackson was a celebrity supernova, brighter by far than any other star,

World leaders wanted to meet him—but Jackson preferred hanging with pals like Macaulay Culkin.

'84

Beat cops: A big fan of police officers, Jackson filmed a video with men and women in uniform.

'85

In a scene out of *A Hard Day's Night*, Jackson wreaked havoc during a stop in London. Being in his presence, says rapper Busta Rhymes, "was so incredibly powerful."

possessed of some supernatural power. "When he did his footwork, he looked like he was hovering about an inch and a half above the ground!" says choreographer Toni Basil, who remembers visiting the set of one of Jackson's videos. "I said, 'My God, the guy levitates when he dances!' It was like he had some kind of energy that took him off the Earth."

What made Michaelmania even more impressive is that Jackson was no typical heartthrob. Defiantly androgynous, resistant to adulthood and outrageously original, he invented a completely unique persona to match his unique talents—and, because of that, found unparalleled adulation. After his moonwalk, adrenalized teens everywhere scurried into their kitchens in socks, trying to master the move; millions more tried to copy his leather-and-rhinestones style (one high school even banned students from wearing a single white glove). That charisma was, for many, utterly mesmerizing. When he went to the Oscars with fellow superstar Madonna, "it was pouring rain, and the limo door opened, and Michael got out first," she recalled, "and *my* bodyguard leaves with Michael under the umbrella. I was left standing in the rain. It was fascinating to see how people responded to him."

Of course nothing stays white-hot forever—supernovas burn out in mere weeks. Jackson's albums *Bad,* in 1987, and *Dangerous,* in 1991, were hits, to be sure, but not nearly as popular as *Thriller.* By the early '90s his eccentric and often troubling behavior began to out-shadow his talent. Dissipated by scandal, disfigured by surgery, he slipped further and further away, finally

"He's a wonderful mover," Fred Astaire once said of Jackson (in Tokyo in '92).

Goofing on his public image, Jackson danced with the Elephant Man's bones in the 1988 video "Leave Me Alone."

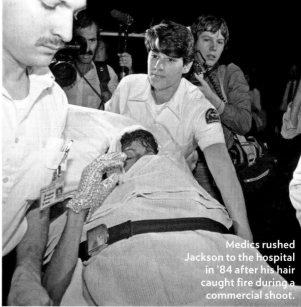

Medics rushed Jackson to the hospital in '84 after his hair caught fire during a commercial shoot.

Full metal jackets: Jackson's signature style was a mix of military tailoring and Liberace glitz.

"He made me believe in magic," rapper Sean "Diddy" Combs says of Jackson (on tour, above, and in the *Smooth Criminal* video).

seeming to vanish altogether inside the walls of Neverland—the fantasy ranch he bought in 1988, back when he was still lighting up the galaxy.

How great, at its peak, was MJ's mojo? Consider how *The New Republic*—an anti-fanzine hardly prone to hype—described the singer in the '80s: He's "the most successful musical performer ever . . . bigger than Sinatra, Elvis, the Beatles, Jesus, Beethoven—all of them." In the end Michael Jackson did something precious few people could ever hope to: He found a way to give the whole world a thrill.

On June 23 Jackson took the stage at the Staples Center in L.A. to rehearse for his tour. "I was so thrilled to see him so happy and so energetic," says Kevin Mazur, the photographer who took this picture. Two days later Jackson was dead.

Everybody Knows Michael

IN HIS GOLDEN MOMENT, EVERYBODY—FROM DI TO SINATRA, RONALD REAGAN AND ANDY WARHOL—WAS SNAPPED WITH THE KING OF POP

'88

When the King of Pop met the Princess of Wales, she requested a favor. Could he possibly sing "Dirty Diana," his song about groupies? Jackson was taken aback. He had purposely left it out of his set as a courtesy, lest people think the tune was about her. "Oh, no! I want you to do it," she replied. And he did, in concert at Wembley, London, in July 1988.

'84

Jackson visited the studio while Frank Sinatra recorded *L.A. Is My Lady* in 1984. The connection: Quincy Jones, fresh off producing Jackson's *Thriller* album, was doing the same honors for Ol' Blue Eyes. "I wanted very much to come to this session," Jackson said. "It's like a dream come true."

Jackson persuaded Marlon Brando to do a cameo in his 2001 video "You Rock My World." Brando also spent time relaxing with the singer at Neverland.

Macaulay Culkin said he bonded with Jackson because they were part of a "unique group" forced to deal with the complications of fame at an early age: "We had a really close relationship. We had this understanding of one another."

Jackson visited the White House in May 1984 and appeared with President Reagan and his wife, Nancy, at an event touting the nation's efforts against drunk driving. Quipped the President: "Well, isn't this a thriller."

"
The way you move,
I think Martians have
invaded your body"

—Elizabeth Taylor, to her
friend Michael Jackson

'85

They met when she walked
out of his concert—but only
because she had lousy seats
and couldn't see the show. He
called her the next day, and
"we talked more and more
on the phone. Then we met
and spent more and more
time with each other and just
became really good friends.
Told each other everything,"
Taylor told Larry King.

In 1984 pop artist Andy Warhol painted Jackson's portrait for the cover of TIME. Today it hangs in the National Portrait Gallery of the Smithsonian Institution in Washington, D.C.

Roll over, Beethoven! Jackson caught up with Chuck Berry, the man who all but invented rock and roll, at a Grammy Awards party. Jackson's father, Joe, who was in an R&B band, played "some of the great early rock and roll and blues songs by Chuck Berry, Little Richard, Otis Redding, you name it," Jackson wrote in his memoir.

In the 1978 TV special *A Special Sesame Street Christmas*, Jackson made a brief appearance, giving Oscar the Grouch a book about ghosts and wishing him a Merry Christmas. Another time, Kermit insisted on a picture with the star.

'02

Britney Spears and
Jackson sang "The Way
You Make Me Feel" on
his 30th anniversary
CBS special and met
again at the 2002 MTV
Video Music Awards.

"There was an identification between Michael and I," Diana Ross once told *Rolling Stone*. "I was older. He kind of idolized me, and he wanted to sing like me."

"He's so magic," Jackson said of James Brown, who performed in some of the same venues as the Jackson 5. "I'd be in the wings when I was like 6 or 7. I'd sit there and watch him."

"I remember my childhood as mostly work, even though I loved to sing," Jackson wrote in his autobiography. "I did it because I enjoyed it and because it was as natural to me as drawing a breath and exhaling it."

Motown's Boy Wonder

HE WAS 5, AND HE WAS ELECTRIFYING. FROM THE BEGINNING WITH HIS FAMILY BAND, THE JACKSON 5, MICHAEL MADE PERFORMING SEEM AS EASY AS ABC, AS SIMPLE AS DO-RE-MI

"We all started singing together after Tito started messin' with Dad's guitar and singin' with the radio," Michael told TIME. "We practiced a lot, and then we started entering talent shows, and we won every one we entered."

Before he was Michael Jackson, he was Little Michael Jackson, a charismatic bundle of energy who made little girls scream and cash registers ring. How did he feel about it? "I was only 5 years old. . . . I remember singing at the top of my voice and dancing with real joy and working too hard for a child," Jackson wrote in *Moonwalk,* his 1988 autobiography. "I do remember the Jackson 5 really taking off when I was only 8 or 9."

Indeed. Five brothers from Gary, Ind., electrified pop music with an upbeat style, solid harmonies and just the right amount of cute. They played six nights a week at Mr. Lucky's, a local club, before moving on to Chicago and New York City, where they dazzled the crowd at Harlem's Apollo Theater. Jackie, Jermaine, Tito and Marlon were all older, but it was Little Michael who mesmerized the crowd, dancing like James Brown and belting out love songs with the authority of a

'69

The brothers moved to California following their initial success, staying with Motown chief Berry Gordy and Diana Ross before the rest of the family arrived and settled in a new home. In 1969 they hit the beach at Paradise Cove.

R&B veteran five or 10 times his age. "He was so energetic that at 5 years old he was like a leader," Jackie told *Rolling Stone.* "We saw that. So we said, 'Hey, Michael, you be the lead guy.' The audience ate it up."

So did the music business. "Michael did a falsetto, a 9-year-old singing, 'I'm a big boy now, looking for a girl to love,'" remembered Ben Brown, who produced the group's first record, "Big Boy," in 1967. "People would throw money onto the stage at concerts. Sometimes he had so much money in his pockets he could hardly hold his pants up."

Singer Gladys Knight caught Michael and his brothers at a Chicago talent show and again at the Apollo. "He had an enormous gift," Knight recalled. She recommended the group to Motown Records chief Berry Gordy, who signed them and, according to *Moonwalk,* promised that their first three records would be No. 1 hits. "I Want You Back," "ABC" and "The Love You Save" all topped the charts—as did their next single, "I'll Be There."

The change in the family's fortunes was breathtaking. In the beginning, dad Joseph Jackson had been a crane operator in a Gary steel mill; his wife, Katherine, worked at Sears. Both loved music and had encouraged the kids to sing and play instruments. "I'm told that my great-great-grandfather was a slave, and he used to sing in the church in Russell County, Ala., where I was born," Katherine said years later, pondering the Jackson 5's success. "He had such a wonderful voice, they said, so powerful and so strong, it would just ring out over everybody else's. And when I heard this, I said to myself, 'Well, maybe it is in the blood.'"

Maybe it was. All nine Jackson children—Rebbie, Jackie, Tito, Jermaine, LaToya, Marlon, Michael, Randy and Janet—had careers in music, thanks in part to their parents. They shared a modest home.

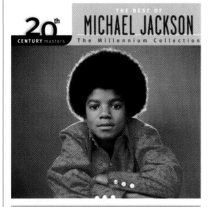

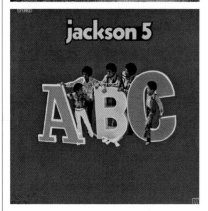

Complex harmonies and intricate routines made fans want to dance. Lyrics like "Sit down girl! I think I love you! No! Get up, girl! Show me what you can do!" (from "ABC") made them want to smile.

He had a hunger to . . . be the best and was willing to work as hard and as long as it took"

—Berry Gordy

"Our family's house in Gary was tiny, only three rooms really, but at the time it seemed much larger to me," Michael remembered. Still, "we always had instruments in the house—a saxophone, a guitar, a trombone—and the kids would help themselves, or sometimes they would sing with us," recalled Katherine. She started their training early. "My first memories are of her holding me and singing songs like "You Are My Sunshine" and "Cotton Fields," said Michael. "She sang to me and to my brothers and sisters often."

Joseph Jackson pushed his sons to be successful—and sometimes, Michael recalled, pushed far too hard. "If you messed up, you got hit, sometimes with a belt, sometimes with a switch," he wrote in *Moonwalk*. "We had a turbulent relationship." There were other downsides as well. "Once I got off-stage,

'75

Stylistically the Jackson 5 (from left, Tito, Jackie, Michael, Jermaine and Marlon) embraced—nay, embodied—the glory that was the '70s.

"I'd like to branch out into things that will give me longevity, perhaps choreography or writing songs for other people," Jackson (in 1972) told PEOPLE.

Hello, California: Jackie, Michael, Randy (standing), Jermaine, Marlon and Tito Jackson relax by the fireplace—and their gold records—in 1972. In the driveway, Michael and Marlon play a little one-on-one.

> 66
>
> Whenever I was little, any
> music would start, they
> couldn't sit me down. They
> couldn't tie me down
> actually. Even to this day, if
> anyone played a beat,
> I'll start kicking in and making
> counter rhythms to
> the beat that I'm hearing"
>
> —Michael Jackson

I was like, very sad," Michael told Oprah Winfrey in 1993. "I would do my schooling, which was three hours with a tutor, and right after that I would go to the recording studio and record, and I'd record for hours and hours until it's time to go to sleep. And I remember . . . there was a park across the street and I'd see all the children playing . . . and I would cry. It would make me sad that I would have to go and work instead."

After the initial hits, the Jackson 5 scored again with "I'll Be There," "Mama's Pearl," "Never Can Say Goodbye," "Maybe Tomorrow" and "Sugar Daddy." Michael also began releasing songs on his own, including Top 10 singles like "Rockin' Robin," "Got To Be There" and, in 1972, "Ben"— an ode to a rat (and the theme to a horror film) which became the first of more than a dozen No. 1 hits for Michael as a solo artist. Despite his growing fame, Michael later told Oprah that his brothers were not jealous that he got most of the attention. "I think they were always happy for me that I could do certain things, but I've never felt jealousy among them."

Television loved the Jackson 5 in the 1970s.

Katherine and Joe Jackson accompanied their son Michael to the Golden Globe Awards in 1973. "Ben," his first No.1 single as a solo artist, won that year's Best Original Song prize.

> ❝ People come up to me and say, 'Well, how's Michael?' or, 'Are you Michael's mother?' and I say, 'I'm mother to all of them'"

—Katherine Jackson

Janet Jackson posed with her beloved big brother at their Hollywood Hills home in 1972. After his death, she told a BET Awards audience, "To you, Michael is an icon. To us, Michael is family."

LaToya Jackson and her brother dressed sharp for the 1972 NAACP Image Awards in L.A.

They appeared on everything from *The Ed Sullivan Show* to *Soul Train,* and for two seasons ABC aired a Jackson 5 cartoon show. Despite Michael's solo success, the brothers stuck together as an act when they left Motown Records in 1976 for CBS Records—with the exception of Jermaine, who had married Berry Gordy's daughter Hazel and decided to remain with his father-in-law's business. Little brother Randy took Jermaine's place and the group had several more hits into the 1980s, including "Shake Your Body (Down to the Ground)" and "State of Shock."

After Michael's solo career flew into the stratosphere, the brothers regrouped for an occasional album or concert tour. But the only Jackson to even approach Michael's success was the baby of the family, Janet Jackson, who has sold more than 100 million records in a career that stretches from 1982 to the present day.

With the exception of an occasional family squabble, Michael remained on good terms with his mother, brothers and sisters. And he worked on improving his relationship with his father. "I love my father, but I don't know him." he told Oprah in 1993. "Am I angry with him? Sometimes I do get angry. I don't know him the way I'd like to know him. My mother's wonderful. To me she's perfection. I just wish I could understand my father."

"I still got Indiana soul in me," the Jackson 5 sang in "Going Back to Indiana." Their childhood home in Gary likely nurtured it.

'02

This image—taken during a 2002 civil trial over canceled concert dates—announced to the world that Jackson's fascination with plastic surgery had reached an alarming level.

And Then Things Got...Weird

AT FIRST, WITH THE ANIMALS AND AMUSEMENT PARK, JACKSON SEEMED SIMPLY TO BE LIVING EVERY KID'S FANTASY. BUT THE SURGERY—AND ODD FRIENDSHIPS—RAISED QUESTIONS

By the time *Off the Wall* and *Thriller* made him a superstar, Michael Jackson had been in the public eye for more than 15 years and had been photographed millions of times. Yet he seldom gave interviews, didn't go to clubs, never voiced a political opinion. He was seen to be very shy, very private and very talented.

And then . . . things happened. Little things at first. Things that made people go *hmmmmmmmmm*. Jackson began buying pets—lots of pets, including two giant pythons, a llama, a giraffe and a chimp named Bubbles, who learned to moonwalk and became Jackson's constant companion. Rumors surfaced that Michael had offered $1 million to buy the Elephant Man's bones, had proposed marriage to Elizabeth Taylor and, in hopes of living to be 150, had taken to sleeping in a hyperbaric oxygen chamber (the *National Enquirer,*

as proof, even published a picture of Jackson inside such a device). Socially his friendships seemed innocent but odd: Although Jackson was in his early 20s, his playmates of choice were children, including *Home Alone* star Macaulay Culkin and tiny Emmanuel Lewis, star of the ABC sitcom *Webster,* whom he carried around like a cute, talking accessory.

And then—bit by bit, nostril by chin-cleft—came the plastic surgery. The

Jackson under glass: A picture of Jackson sleeping in a hyperbaric oxygen chamber led to reports that he was using it to prolong his life. He later said he was simply testing the machine at a hospital burn center he helped finance.

results, modest at first, became over time undeniably bizarre.

So what was going on? It wasn't always easy to tell: Jackson, a master showman, knew the publicity value of gossip and mystery. Years later an *Enquirer* reporter claimed that Jackson's people had given them the oxygen-chamber picture and told them the only requirement for printing it was that *Enquirer* use the word "bizarre" in their article. Jackson himself told a different story to Oprah Winfrey in 1993. "I did a commercial for Pepsi, and I was burned very badly and we settled for 1 million dollars," he said, adding that he gave the money to an L.A. hospital to build the Michael Jackson Burn Center. When Jackson toured the center, he climbed into the hyperbaric chamber—which is used to speed healing—and "somebody takes the picture.... He made a copy, and these pictures went all over the world with this lie attached to it. It's a complete lie." The Elephant Man's bones? "I love the story of the Elephant Man," Jackson told Winfrey, "but no, I never asked for the . . . where am I going to put some bones? And why would I want some bones?" He did not propose to Elizabeth Taylor, both said, but they were close friends.

As for the surgery: Frank Dileo, Jackson's manager for much of the '80s, confirmed that Jackson had had his nose done, "as every person in Hollywood has," and had had a cleft put in his chin. Why? "He wanted one." And as for his skin lightening as he got older, Jackson told Winfrey that he had a disorder that destroyed his pigmentation and left his face blotchy. Makeup evened it out. And in case you were wondering, Jackson added, "I've never had my cheekbones done, never had my eyes done, never had my lips done."

And the hanging out with young boys? There was no question that Jackson—who liked horror movies, zoos and roller coasters—was, in many ways, a kid himself. "I didn't have a childhood," he said years later. "When you don't have a childhood . . . you try to compensate for the loss."

Double Date: In 1984 Jackson took Emmanuel Lewis and Brooke Shields to the Grammy Awards in Los Angeles.

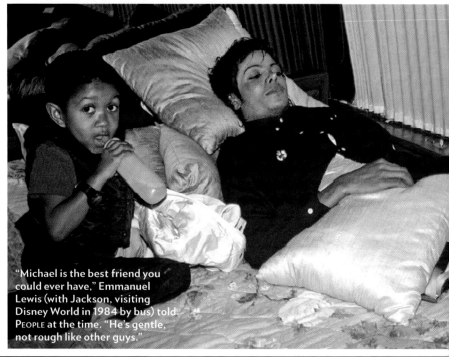

"Michael is the best friend you could ever have," Emmanuel Lewis (with Jackson, visiting Disney World in 1984 by bus) told PEOPLE at the time. "He's gentle, not rough like other guys."

like the old Indian proverb SAYS Do not judge a Man until you've walked 2 moons in his Moccosins.

Most people don't KNow Me, that is wHy they write such ~~rotten~~ things in wich MOST is not TRUe I cry very very often Because it HuRts and I worry about the children all my children all over the World, I live for them.

If a Man could SAy nothing AgAiNST a character but what he can prove, History Could NOT Be Written.

Animals sTRike, not from Malice, But because they want To live, it is the Same with those wHo CRITICIZE, they desire our BLood, NOT our pain. But STill I MusT achieve I MuST seek TRuth in all things. I MuST endure for the power I was sent forth, for the world for the children

BuT HAVe Mercy, for I've been Bleeding a lONg Time NOW. M.J.

To enter Jackson's Neverland bedroom in 1997, one had to pass under two life-size figures: a Boy Scout and a girl wearing a British bobby's hat. Inside toys, gadgets, books, Peter Pan paraphernalia and a Grammy award were on display, along with Sega Saturn and Nintendo 64 video games. At left, a 1984 open letter from Jackson to his critics. "Have mercy," he wrote, "for I've been bleeding a long time now."

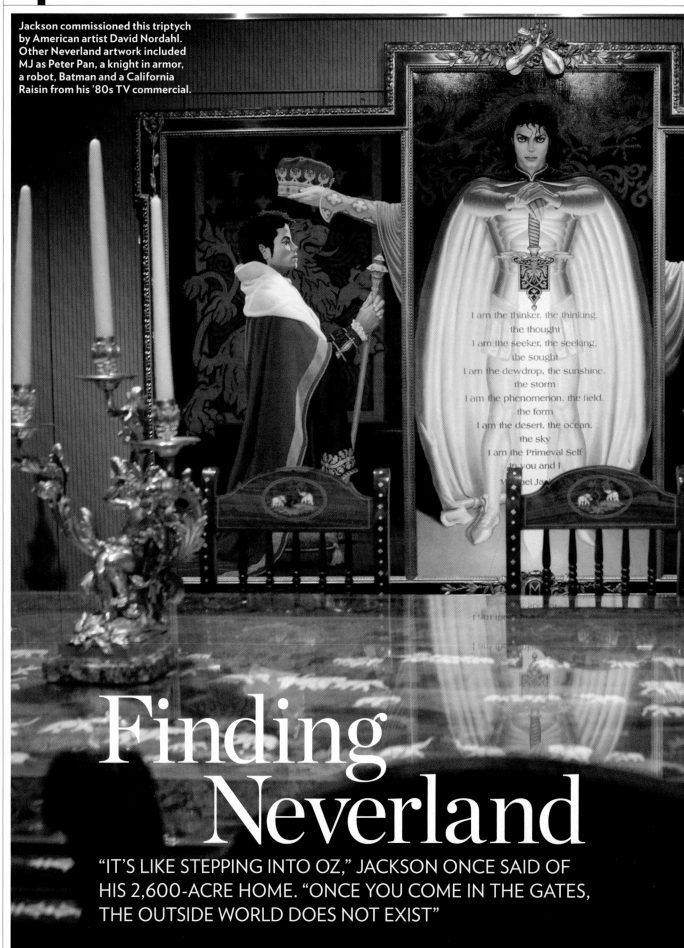

Jackson commissioned this triptych by American artist David Nordahl. Other Neverland artwork included MJ as Peter Pan, a knight in armor, a robot, Batman and a California Raisin from his '80s TV commercial.

I am the thinker, the thinking,
the thought
I am the seeker, the seeking,
the sought
I am the dewdrop, the sunshine,
the storm
I am the phenomenon, the field,
the form
I am the desert, the ocean,
the sky
I am the Primeval Self
In you and I
Michael Ja...

Finding Neverland

"IT'S LIKE STEPPING INTO OZ," JACKSON ONCE SAID OF HIS 2,600-ACRE HOME. "ONCE YOU COME IN THE GATES, THE OUTSIDE WORLD DOES NOT EXIST"

Jackson transformed the 22-building estate, bought for $17 million in 1988, into the fantasy playground he never got to enjoy as a child himself—complete with a zoo, movie theater and amusement park.

Fit for a King

COLLECTIBLES FROM A CANCELED 2009 NEVERLAND AUCTION

SPARKLE IN HIS STEP

"Your eye will go to the light," Michael Bush, one of Jackson's costumers, said by way of explaining why the star covered his dance shoes—and everything else—with rhinestones.

BEHIND THE GLITTER

Stage wear—like the shirt below and the silk-lined, Swarovski-encrusted jacket at left—gave evidence that, as a performer, Jackson was one of the hardest working men in show business.

KING COLLECTOR

Jackson holds crowns, similar to this one trimmed in white-mink fur, in several portraits. Other royalty-themed items in his collection included a ceremonial scepter and a full-length red velvet cape.

ODDS AND ENDS

MJ's collection of figures included a 4-inch tumbling angel, a 6-ft. toy soldier and a life-size Bruce Lee replica.

THE GLOVED ONE'S GLOVES

"I felt that one glove was cool," said Jackson of his single-handed fashion statement. "Wearing two gloves seemed so ordinary."

Metamorphoses

FOUR DECADES, STARDOM AND A SCALPEL: THE CHANGING
FACE OF MICHAEL JOSEPH JACKSON

AGE: ABOUT 12

AGE 45

Whathappened? Hard to say. Jackson never said how, exactly, he created the face he wore; speculation included eyelid lifts, skin bleaching, nose jobs (plural), a chin implant, cheek implants, lip plumping and a wig.

What happened psychologically? Extreme fame, unimaginable wealth, a lost childhood, isolation, lack of education, fading fame, disappearing wealth or perhaps Acute Elvis Syndrome in its most virulent form? In the end no one may have known the real answer—including Michael Jackson.

AGE: ABOUT 6

AGE 14

AGE: ABOUT 21

AGE: ABOUT 34

"

I've never had my cheekbones done, never had my eyes done, never had my lips done . . . [but] I'm never pleased with anything . . . I try not to look in the mirror"

—Michael Jackson, 1993

AGE 37

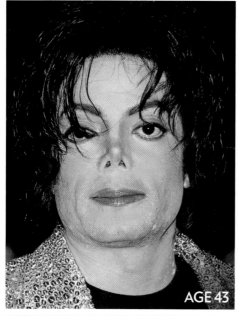

AGE 43

AGE 44

AGE 46

AGE 22

AGE 31

AGE 33

AGE 26

AGE 42

AGE 50

'94

"I am very much in love with Michael; I dedicate my life to being his wife," Lisa Marie Presley said in an Aug. 1, 1994, statement announcing that she had become Mrs. Michael Jackson weeks before. "We both look forward to raising a family."

Love &
Marriages

TWO SURPRISE WEDDINGS DIDN'T PAN OUT, BUT,
DESPITE APPEARANCES, PARENTHOOD MAY HAVE
BEEN JACKSON'S MOST WINNING GROWN-UP ROLE

"People said the MTV kiss was phony," Michael's former publicist said of the famous smooch the newlyweds shared during the 1994 MTV Video Music Awards. "But I think they were in love."

M ichael Jackson deserved the honorific we almost automatically apply to anyone with a CD or two on his résumé: He truly was an artist. He used beats, melody and lyrics to both define his individuality and build a bridge to an audience of billions around the world. But music couldn't hold him—for better and worse, Jackson turned everything into art, expressing himself and often challenging and commenting on his audience's expectations, with his dance routines, his clothes, his plastic surgeries, his extreme dermatology and even, it must be said, his two most public relationships. We will never know how much his marriages were propped up on the traditional pillars of love and children—or to what extent they were meant to enhance his image, bolster his legal position, put him in the spotlight or just mess with our minds. Michael Jackson himself may have not known the real answer.

With Lisa Marie Presley, it is at least possible to point to signs of kinship. Her father had been the biggest star of his era and had buckled under the tremendous weight of his fame, dying in 1977, when she was 9. Like Michael, she knew a lot about fame, public expectations and people who just might like you for your money. They had known each other since childhood, when Elvis took his daughter to meet the Jackson 5, and she had reached out to him in 1993, when he had been accused of molesting a child. Jackson no doubt appreciated the support, but Lisa Marie, with her unique history, also offered something few other women could: As Jackson once said, "I hate to admit it, but I feel strange around everyday people."

The timing, and speed, of their union prompted some cynics to suggest that Jackson, reeling after settling the molestation case out of court in 1994, desperately wanted some good, wholesome publicity. Lisa Marie, 26 at the time, announced her split from her husband, musician Danny Keough—with whom she had two children—in April 1994; she and Jackson, 35, were married before a judge in the Dominican Republic on May 26. Speaking for

"They hold hands, kiss and cuddle, stare into each other's eyes and look at the stars together," said an eyewitness who caught them in honeymoon mode. Despite PDA at Neverland (left), while vacationing in France (above, left) and in Budapest (hanging out with Michael's friend and traveling companion Michu), the public remained incredulous—and unsurprised when the couple broke up 20 months later.

Jackson's family, attorney Johnnie Cochran said everyone was "happily surprised" by the nuptials. Lisa Marie's mother, Priscilla Presley, who had attended Lisa Marie's first wedding but not her second, said through a spokesperson that she was "supportive of everything Lisa Marie does." Although the couple went on to appear in numerous photo ops around the world, they had little to say in public—except, notably, during an ABC TV interview, when Lisa, asked if the couple had sex often, replied with a resounding "yes, yes, yes!"

If the questions about connubial bliss were a bit forward they were also fair. When the marriage ended with Lisa Marie filing for divorce in January 1996, the couple had already established a pattern of living in separate residences, with her often staying in Hidden Hills, a gated California community 90 miles from Neverland. "There are a lot of shady characters around Michael who were upsetting to Lisa," said a source close to Presley. "She felt that in their minds she was part of a machinery to re-create his image." She may also have been frustrated by his refusal to accept her invitations to explore Scientology, which for her had become a spiritual and social center that she thought would be helpful for him in dealing with anger issues that stemmed perhaps from his troubled relationship with his father, Joe. In any case neither seemed especially upset when the marriage ended. She "is not crying in her soup," the source said of Lisa Marie (who has since married and divorced actor Nicolas Cage and married for a fourth time, to musician Michael Lockwood). As for Jackson, he dealt with the divorce in his fashion—by hopping a plane for France and checking into the Sleeping Beauty suite at Euro Disney.

But if Jackson-Presley was at least a merger, as Lisa Marie's lawyer said, "of rock and roll royalty," how to explain Debbie Rowe? A divorced motorcycle enthusiast, Jackson's second wife personified that "everyday person" that he said made him uncomfortable. Yet Jackson and she had been friends for some 15 years after meeting in his dermatologist's office, where Rowe worked. Described by a friend as "a great

Pregnant when she married Jackson in 1996, Debbie Rowe, who bore two of his three children, soon moved from a one-bedroom apartment into a $1.27 million L.A. home.

'01

"I was struck," a source said of Michael's three children, "by how considerate and nice and normal they all were." The two oldest, Paris and Prince, posed with Dad in 2001 for a rare photo shoot without veils.

rescuer," Rowe, now 50, and Jackson were married in 1996. "I'm doing a favor for a good friend," Rowe said, explaining her motives when her decision to bear Jackson's children became public. "I had them because I wanted him to be a father," she told Britain's GMTV. "I didn't do it to be a mother."

Rowe has said that she is no gold-digger and wanted to give Jackson children "as a present." Publicly, it has never been clear whether Jackson is the biological father of the two children—Prince Michael Jackson, now 12, and Paris Michael Katherine, 11—to whom she gave birth. The role he played in the birth of his third child, Prince Michael II, 7, and nicknamed Blanket—born to an unnamed surrogate mother—is also not known. Under oath at Jackson's 2005 trial for child molestation, Rowe, who was divorced from him in 1999, said she had not met her own children until they were 3 or 4. "It's an unusual family," the psychic Uri Geller, a Jackson friend, once said, stating the obvious.

With one famous exception—the time he dangled Blanket over the balcony of a Berlin hotel in 2002—Jackson was never accused of being a poor father. He took his children around the world with him—albeit wearing masks and veils—his sincere intention being to protect the kids from paparazzi and potential kidnappers. When he died on June 25, Jackson left his children to uncertain futures. With their father gone and Rowe having once relinquished her parental rights (they were later restored), it is unclear who will raise them. Rowe, now single and raising horses in Palmdale, Calif., was said to be "inconsolable" and not able to decide if she wanted to pursue custody, though her lawyer insisted she retained that option.

In the meantime the children are in the care of Michael's mother, Katherine, who has been granted temporary custody. She was the only member of the clan to come to her troubled son's 2005 child-molestation trial every day. At 79, grandma Jackson clearly knows something about motherhood as a lifetime commitment.

Oldest son Prince, 12, strolled with Dad in L.A. on June 3.

"He does it for when they go out," Michael's mom said of the veils and masks often worn by his kids. "He's afraid somebody's going to kidnap them." Left: Prince, Paris and Blanket in 2008.

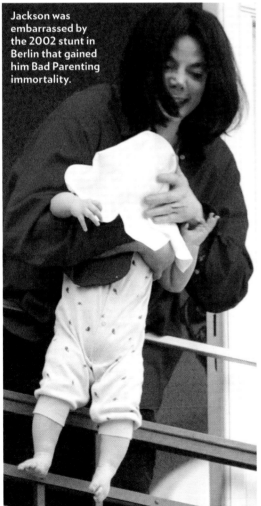

Jackson was embarrassed by the 2002 stunt in Berlin that gained him Bad Parenting immortality.

'03

In October 2003, more than 35 years after Michael Jackson and his four older brothers became the Jackson 5, the extended family gathered at his Neverland Ranch.

'05

Staggered by the accusations against him and the emotional toll of his grueling 14-week trial, Jackson, accompanied by his father, Joe (right), arrived at court in March 2005, dazed and disoriented.

Michael on trial

ACCUSED BUT NOT CONVICTED, JACKSON NEVER FULLY RECOVERED FROM A PAIR OF SCANDALS THAT LEFT HIM REELING AND FANS WONDERING

The year 1993 started brilliantly for Jackson, who on Jan. 31 rocked the Super Bowl halftime show with a smashing version of his hit "Heal the World." By the end of summer, though, his star would fall rapidly through the pop cultural firmament, and Jackson's world would need healing in ways he perhaps had never imagined.

The bad news broke on Aug. 24, when a Beverly Hills dentist publicly accused Jackson of molesting his then-13-year-old son. Jackson, who was in Bangkok kicking off the third leg of his Dangerous tour, vehemently denied the allegations but soon canceled concerts citing "acute dehydration." Weeks later, while announcing a multimillion-dollar lawsuit against the star alleging sexual battery, seduction, fraud and negligence, the father put forth an unsettling tale of Jackson's obsession with his son. The boy had simply been a fan until 1992 when, his father said, Jackson began paying him visits, sending him gifts and ultimately inviting him to Neverland. The boy, his father said, could even offer a detailed description of Jackson's genitals.

When the charges became public, Jackson tried to make a case for himself as an innocent man-child, letting it be known through insiders in his camp that sharing a bed with young male house guests was

for him just an innocent pastime. But his record of concert cancellations—across several continents and most notably in Puerto Rico, where he might have come under American legal jurisdiction and been subject to arrest—suggested inner turmoil. In November Jackson canceled the last month of the tour because, he said, "I was humiliated, embarrassed, hurt and suffering great pain in my heart."

By then Jackson had jetted off to Europe with Elizabeth Taylor and her then-husband, Larry Fortensky; Jackson's lawyers said he had entered drug rehab after abusing prescription medication. In December the LAPD arrived at Neverland with a warrant. Said a former Jackson repre-

A year after a young fan (foreground) and his sister were his guests in Monaco, Jackson reportedly paid their family $20 million to settle a suit accusing him of having molested the boy during sleepovers at Neverland.

"I am totally innocent of any wrongdoing," Jackson said in a 1993 broadcast. When he was booked on similar charges 10 years later, his mug shot (right) seemed to express the ravages of scandal.

Live from Neverland Valley

Santa Barbara County Sheriff's Dept.

11/20/2003
Photo Image of:
NAME: JACKSON, MICHAEL
RAC: B
DOB: 8/29/1958   SEX: M
HGT: 511   AGE: 45
BLD: WGT: 120
HAI: BLK   CMP:
MKS: EYE: BRO
BOOKING #:   621785

sentative: "Whether he will continue to be the worldwide phenomenon he once was is very doubtful."

Jackson fought back by addressing a prime-time American TV audience from his home via satellite on Dec. 22. Appearing calm and speaking in his familiar soft voice, he said, "Don't treat me like a criminal, because I am innocent." Johnnie Cochran, the lawyer who would later work a miracle for O.J. Simpson, took over Jackson's defense. For Cochran it did not look like *Mission Impossible*: After ques-

tioning some 200 witnesses, two grand juries had not found sufficient evidence to support the boy's charges, and a phone poll conducted by *A Current Affair* showed 80 percent of viewers did not believe him. Still, perhaps because the stakes were too high—if convicted on criminal charges, Jackson might have spent a decade or more in prison—Jackson caved, and the parties announced on Jan. 25 that they had settled the suit for an amount later reported to be some $20 million. Because of the boy's refusal to testi-

fy, the police declined to pursue the criminal case, and Jackson issued the obligatory statement about wanting to get on with his life.

Jackson's second child-molestation scandal seemed like an eerie echo of the first. The chief difference was that instead of being *accused* of spending time in bed with young boys, Jackson showed up in a February 2003 ABC TV documentary saying plainly that he was still having the slumber parties that got him in trouble 10 years earlier. In *Living with Michael Jackson*, British journalist Martin Bashir capitalized on the eight months of access the singer had inexplicably given him to get Jackson on the record about his plastic surgery ("Just my nose . . . honestly") his personal worth ("Is it over a billion dollars?" "Yes") and his relationship with a 12-year-old cancer survivor. The film, seen by 27 million viewers, showed Jackson cuddling and holding hands with the boy and talking about how he had "slept in a bed with many children." Santa

Jackson was feeling feisty during a 2002 breach-of-contract suit. After testifying that he couldn't remember details of a 1999 concert deal, a lawyer asked if he suffered memory loss. "Not that I can recall," he said.

> **"**
> Why not? If you're going to be a pedophile . . . [or] Jack the Ripper . . . it's not a good idea. That I am not"
>
> —Michael Jackson, on *60 Minutes*, when asked if he thought it was okay to let children sleep in his bed

Jackson (arriving at court in March 2005) would leave with an even bigger smile after being acquitted on all counts. He would spend most of his remaining years in self-imposed exile in the Middle East and Europe.

Barbara D.A. Thomas Sneddon—the same prosecutor who had probed Jackson in 1993—launched an investigation. On Nov. 18, 2003, California authorities conducted a showy raid on Neverland and confiscated computers, photographs and videotapes. In December Jackson was formally charged with child molestation and was free on $3 million bail.

The trial that began in earnest Feb. 28, 2005, was long (14 weeks), predictably bizarre (Jackson arrived more than an hour late one day, wearing a suit jacket and pajama bottoms) and relentlessly sordid. The boy, then 14, told a tale of being plied with pornography and wine, which Jackson, he said, called "Jesus juice." He also said that Jackson had performed sexual acts with him and had extolled masturbation as a way of keeping men from raping women.

Understandably, perhaps, it was not a very confident-looking Jackson who shambled into the courthouse carrying an umbrella (his skin he said was hypersensitive to the sun) to hear testimony that the accuser's fingerprints were found on a copy of Jackson's *Barely Legal* magazine. Jackson did not testify on his own behalf, but offered a race-based defense in a radio interview with the Rev. Jesse Jackson. "I'm totally innocent and it's just very painful," he said. "There has been kind of a pattern among black luminaries in this country."

Jackson received strong support in court from his old pal Macaulay Culkin, who had enjoyed sleepovers with the singer and testified that their relationship had been G-rated. The defense also called as witnesses several parents of Jackson's house guests, who spoke of his generosity. But Jackson may have been helped most by a sad parade of hangers-on—some of whom, in the process of condemning him, admitted they had peddled dirt about his lifestyle to the tabloids.

For Jackson's legal team, the boy's mother—though called by the prosecution—turned out to be, in the words of *Vanity Fair* writer Maureen Orth, "the gift that keeps on giving." At one point the defense introduced an 80-minute tape that showed her clowning, preening for the camera—and praising Jackson. On June 13, 2005, the jury found Jackson not guilty on all counts. Jackson had dodged a possible 20-year sentence and was cheered by fans outside the courthouse, but he was no winner, having lost his privacy and whatever was left of his career momentum. For Jackson, the child-molestation scandals were a one-two punch from which he would never fully recover.

Global Mourning

A MASS MOONWALK IN PARIS, A VIGIL IN HARLEM, INMATES DANCING
IN ASIA: AROUND THE WORLD, FANS HONORED THE KING OF POP

CHENGDU, CHINA
Fans hold a candlelight
vigil for Jackson on June
26. The singer never
performed in mainland
China, but he was one of
the first western artists
whose music was made
available there.

> **❝**
>
> I don't think anyone can
>
> be indifferent to
>
> Michael Jackson. . . . I will
>
> enormously miss his voice, his
>
> songs and his presence"
>
> —French First Lady Carla Bruni-Sarkozy

We have a gentleman here *that needs help and he's not breathing*," says the caller, an unidentified man. "*We're trying to pump him . . . he's not responding to anything.*"

It is 12:21 p.m., June 25, and Michael Jackson is the man who needs help. The next two hours are chaos: An ambulance races him to Ronald Reagan UCLA Medical Center in Los Angeles; doctors try frantically to revive him; reports about his condition begin to swirl. At 2:26 p.m., an era ends: The King of Pop is declared dead. "It feels like when Kennedy died," the singer Celine Dion will later say. "When Elvis Presley died."

The night before, Jackson had been onstage at

the Staples Center in L.A., rehearsing with backup dancers for his upcoming concert tour. The practice was grueling, and Jackson's dancing was sharp and strenuous. "He did the moonwalk—everything!" says Michael Bush, a costume designer and one of some 30 staffers watching in the otherwise empty arena.

Then, on June 25, Jackson awoke, complained of feeling weak and went back to bed. His personal physician, Conrad Murray, who had stayed overnight at Jackson's rented Holmby Hills mansion, found the singer unconscious in his bedroom. Murray performed CPR and yelled for security to call 911. Too late: Says one source: Jackson's "face had no life."

An autopsy by the L.A. County coroner's office yielded no cause of death. And with toxicology tests

DETROIT
Many vigils, such as this one in the city where the Jackson 5 recorded on the Motown label, were a mix of celebration and sadness.

PARIS
A giant banner unfurled beneath the Eiffel Tower. French Culture Minister Frédéric Mitterrand said, "We all have a little bit of Michael Jackson in us."

APOLLO
MICHAEL JACKSON MEMORIAL OPEN HOUSE
FREE PUBLIC CELEBRATION
Tuesday, June 30, 2009
Stop in from 2pm - 8pm,
Last Group Entry 6pm

HARLEM
Thousands gathered outside the theater where Jackson sang as a child. One mourner there said of his idol, "He has inspired me to be who I am today."

MICHAEL JACKSON

CHENGDU
Some brought flowers for their fallen star. One fan in Shanghai said on his Facebook page, "Everyone in this world will miss you! We love you Michael!"

still weeks away, speculation about Jackson's drug use ran wild. His close friend Deepak Chopra said Jackson's 2005 child-molestation trial—he was acquitted—so stressed him that he relied on painkillers for relief. Doctors "gave him drugs instead of managing the stress," Chopra said. Another source told PEOPLE Jackson received a daily injection of the painkiller Demerol.

The matter of whether or not drug abuse caused Jackson's death—and if so, who enabled him—was unlikely to be resolved anytime soon. Nor would the issue of Jackson's complicated finances. He sold some 750 million albums worldwide and partly owned a music catalogue worth close to $2 billion, yet still reportedly had debts of nearly $500 million. And what about his three children—son Prince Michael I, 12, daughter Paris, 11, and son Prince Michael II, 7, known as Blanket? Who would take care of them? Jackson's mother, Katherine, 79, was granted temporary guardianship, and the children moved in with her and their grandfather Joe Jackson, 80. But their future too would remain up in the air for some time.

None of that mattered much to the throngs that turned out around the globe to mourn Michael. As the news spread, crowds gathered everywhere to commiserate, sing, dance—even stage a mass moonwalk, as happened in Paris, London, Vienna and Beirut. In Paris they flocked to the Eiffel Tower and rendered a tuneful "Billie Jean"; in a Filipino prison, inmates danced to "I'll Be There."

Michael had wanted very much for his children to see him perform live—to get some sense of his glory days. Now they won't get to see him dance onstage. But they will know how much the world cared.

A child leaves a keepsake outside the gates of Jackson's rented home in Holmby Hills, Calif.

Some mourners in Argentina copied Jackson's signature outfits and moves during their tribute to the pop star.

Within hours of his death, fans flocked to Jackson's small childhood home in Gary, Ind. Some formed a prayer circle; others left teddy bears and flowers. One town resident said of Jackson, "Ever since I was a kid, I was dancing and singing like him."

Michael's sister Janet made a surprise appearance at the BET Awards in Los Angeles just three days after her brother's death. "My entire family wanted to be here tonight, but it was just too painful," she told the crowd. "We miss him so much."

Farewell

"I hate to take credit for the songs I've written. I feel that somewhere, someplace, it's been done, and I'm just a courier bringing it into the world. I really believe that. I love what I do"

—Michael Jackson

1958–2009

MASTHEAD

EDITOR Cutler Durkee **DESIGN DIRECTOR** Sara Williams **DIRECTOR OF PHOTOGRAPHY** Chris Dougherty **ART DIRECTOR** Cass Spencer **DESIGNERS** Stephen Bamonte, Wilbert Gutierrez, Margarita Mayoral-Medina, Suzanne Noli **EDITORIAL MANAGER** Andrew Abrahams **PHOTOGRAPHY EDITOR** C. Tiffany Lee- Ramos **PHOTO RESEARCHERS** Jen Lombardo, James Miller, Linda Pacheco **WRITERS** Steve Dougherty, Charles Leerhsen, Larry Sutton, Alex Tresniowski, Kara Warner **REPORTERS** Sabrina Ford, Lesley Messer, Gail Nussbaum, Ellen Shapiro, Mary Shaughnessy, Jane Sugden **COPY EDITORS** Ben Harte (Chief), Jennifer Broughel, Aura Davies, Alan Levine, Amanda Pennelly, Mary Radich **PRODUCTION ARTISTS** Denise M. Doran, Ilsa Enomoto, Cynthia Miele, Daniel J. Neuburger **SCANNERS** Brien Foy, Stephen Pabarue **IMAGING** Francis Fitzgerald (Director), Rob Roszkowski (Manager), Charles Guardino, Romeo Cifelli, Jeffrey Ingledue **SPECIAL THANKS TO** David Barbee, Jane Bealer, Stacie Fenster, Margery Frohlinger, Ean Sheehy, Céline Wojtala, Patrick Yang

TIME INC. HOME ENTERTAINMENT PUBLISHER Richard Fraiman **GENERAL MANAGER** Steven Sandonato **EXECUTIVE DIRECTOR MARKETING SERVICES** Carol Pittard **DIRECTOR RETAIL & SPECIAL SALES** Tom Mifsud **DIRECTOR NEW PRODUCT DEVELOPMENT** Peter Harper **ASSISTANT DIRECTOR BOOKAZINE MARKETING** Laura Adam **ASSISTANT PUBLISHING DIRECTOR BRAND MARKETING** Joy Butts **ASSOCIATE COUNSEL** Helen Wan **BOOK PRODUCTION MANAGER** Susan Chodakiewicz **DESIGN & PREPRESS MANAGER** Anne-Michelle Gallero **BRAND & LICENSING MANAGER** Alexandra Bliss **ASSISTANT BRAND MANAGER** Melissa Joy Kong **SPECIAL THANKS TO** Christine Austin, Glenn Buonocore, Jim Childs, Rose Cirrincione, Jacqueline Fitzgerald, Lauren Hall, Jennifer Jacobs, Suzanne Janso, Brynn Joyce, Mona Li, Robert Marasco, Amy Migliaccio, Brooke Reger, Dave Rozzelle, Ilene Schreider, Adriana Tierno, Alex Voznesenskiy, Sydney Webber, Jonathan White

ISBN 10: 1-60320-131-9
ISBN 13: 978-1-60320-131-5
Library of Congress Control Number: 2009931795
Copyright © 2009 Time Inc. Home Entertainment.
Published by People Books, Time Inc., 1271 Avenue of the Americas, New York, N.Y. 10020. All rights reserved.

We welcome your comments and suggestions about People Books. **Please write to us at People Books,** Attention: Book Editors, P.O. Box 11016, Des Moines, IA 50336-1016.
● If you would like to order any of our hardcover Collectors Edition books, please call us at 1-800-327-6388 (Monday through Friday, 7 a.m.-8 p.m., or Saturday, 7 a.m.-6 p.m. Central Time).

CREDITS

Front Cover
Kevin Mazur/Wireimage

Title Page
Bobby Holland/MPTV

Contents
2 Jim Britt/Shooting Star

Gallery
4 Greg Allen/Retna; **6** Lynn Goldsmith; **8-9** Kevin Mazur/Wireimage (3); **10** Reuters; **12** Sam Emerson/Polaris; **14** Harry Benson; **16** Stephen Vaughan/Sipa; **18** Harry Benson; **20** Harry Benson; **22** Dilip Mehta/ Contact Press Images; **25** Harry Benson; **26** Dilip Mehta/ Contact Press Images; **28** MR Photo/Corbis; **30-31** Herb Ritts/Lime Foto (2)

SuperStar
32 Ebet Roberts/ Redferns/Getty Images; **34** (clockwise from top left) Reed Saxon/AP; Nick Elgar/London Features International; Everett; **35** Sam Emerson/Polaris; **36** Dave Hogan/Getty Images; **38** (clockwise from left) Polaris; Zuma; Bettmann/Corbis; Polaris; **39** (from top) Harrison Funk/Zuma; Entertainment Pictures/ Zuma; **40** Kevin Mazur/ AEG/Wireimage

Famous Friends
42 Rex USA; **44** (clockwise from top) Ed Thrasher/MPTV; Polaris; Ernie McCreight/Rex USA; **45** Michael Evans/ Zuma; **47** Polaris; **48** (from top) Corbis; Globe; **49** Jim Britt/Shooting Star; **50** Kevin Mazur/ Wireimage; **51** (from top) Julian Wasser/ Getty Images; Kevork Djansezian/AP

Growing Up
52 Henry Diltz; **53** Michael Ochs Archive/ Getty Images; **54** Lawrence Schiller © Polaris Communications; **57** Fin Costello/Redferns/ Getty Images; **58** (from top) Gunther/MPTV; Neal Preston/Corbis; **59** AP; **60** Fotos International/

Getty Images; **61** (from top) Michael Ochs Archive/Getty Images; Phil Roach/IPOL/Globe; Tammie Arroyo/AFF

Things Get Weird
62 Ramey; **63** AP; **64** (from top) Ron Galella/ Wireimage; Polaris; **65** (from top) Harry Benson; Todd Gold

Neverland
66 Nancy Pastor/Polaris; **67** (from top) Stewart Cook/Rex USA; Shaan Kokin/Julien's Auctions/ Rex USA; Paul Buck/EPA/ Corbis; **68-69** Henry Leutwyler/August Images (10)

Is That You?
70 MPTV; **71** Carlo Allegri/Getty Images; **72** (clockwise from top left) People Picture/ Capital Pictures/Retna; Photoshot/Admedia; Michael Ochs Archive/ Getty Images; Andrew Shawaf/Online USA/ Getty Images; Aaron

Lambert/Getty Images; Lester Cohen/AP; Gilbert Flores/Celebrity Photo; Neal Preston/Corbis; **73** (clockwise from top left) Dave Hogan/Getty Images; Polaris; Janet Gough/Celebrity Photo; Matt Baron/BEImages; Chris-Jason/National Photo Group; Neal Preston/Corbis

Family Man
74 Ken Goff/Globe; **76** Reuters; **77** (clockwise from top left) Photo B.D.V./Corbis; Sichov-Niviere/Sipa; Kim Kulish/ AFP/Getty Images; **78** Jonathan Exley/Contour by Getty Images; **79** Reuters; **80** Splash News; **81** (clockwise from top left) Mike/National Photo Group; Fabrizio Bensch/ Reuters; X 17; Reuters; **82** Jonathan Exley/Contour by Getty Images

On Trial
84 Kimberly White/ Reuters; **85** Nikos

Vinieratos/Rex USA; **86** (clockwise from top left) Reuters; CNP/Corbis; Ed Souza/Santa Maria Times/Zuma (2); **87** Mike Eliason/Santa Barbara News-Press/Zuma

A Sudden Loss
88 Zheng Duo/Color China Photos/Zuma; **90-91** (clockwise from left) Julien Hekimian/ Wireimage; Nancy Pastor/ Polaris; Mary Altaffer/AP; Timothy Fadek/Polaris; **92** (from top) Kevin Winter/Getty Images; Phil McCarten/Reuters; Tasos Katopodis/Getty Images; **93** (from top) Enrique Marcarian/Reuters; Zheng Duo/Color China Photos/Zuma

Farewell
Dilip Mehta/Contact Press Images

This Page
Jim Britt/Shooting Star

Back Cover
Kevin Mazur/Wireimage (3)